DAILY LIFE IN A
PLAINS
INDIAN
VILLAGE
1868

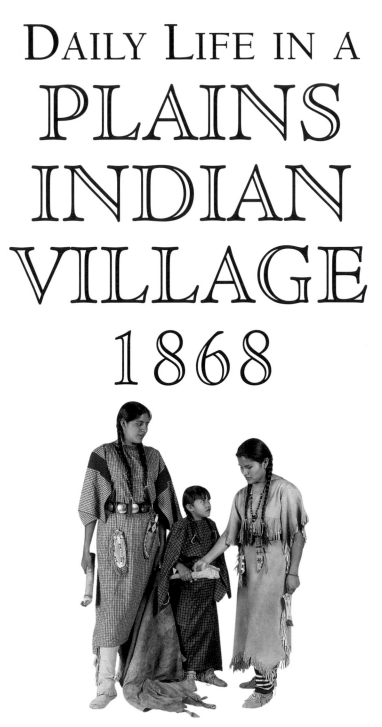

MICHAEL BAD HAND TERRY

Clarion Books

To my parents, Buck and Faye,
who gave me the freedom and courage to follow my dreams.

Clarion Books
a Houghton Mifflin Company imprint
215 Park Avenue South, New York, New York 10003

Copyright © 1999 by Breslich & Foss Ltd

First published in the United States in 1999 by Clarion Books,
a Houghton Mifflin Company imprint.

First published in Great Britain in 1999 by Heinemann Library, a division of
Reed Educational and Professional Publishing Limited

For information about permission to reproduce selections from this book,
write to Permissions, Houghton Mifflin Company, 215 Park Avenue South, New York, NY 10003.

Printed in Hong Kong
First American Edition

Library of Congress Cataloging-in-Publication Data
available on request

10 9 8 7 6 5 4 3 2 1

Conceived and produced by Breslich & Foss Ltd, London
Series Editor: Laura Wilson
Art Director: Nigel Osborne
Design: Phil Richardson
Photography: Miki Slingsby

CONTENTS

WHO WERE THE PLAINS INDIANS?

Plains Indian council meeting, 1878

More than 14,000 years ago the ancestors of the Plains Indians migrated from Asia to North America, where many of them settled in the upper Mississippi River and Great Lakes areas. Displaced from their land by Europeans who came to settle in the east, they moved to the central plains (*see map opposite*).

Most of the Plains Indians were nomadic, which means that they were not farmers who stayed in one place and raised crops on the land but hunter-gatherers who moved about, getting their food by killing buffalo from the large herds that grazed the prairies and by trading goods with other tribes.

In the mid-1880s, as immigrants and settlers began to come from the east, traveling westward in covered wagons and claiming some of the Plains Indians territory for themselves, the U.S. Army began to build forts in these areas. Relations between the Plains Indians and the white settlers grew increasingly tense, and a series of misunderstandings eventually led to the massacre of an Indian village. This marked the beginning of more than thirty years of war between the Plains Indians and the U.S. Army. Within five years of the Sioux and Cheyenne victory at the Battle of the Little Bighorn in 1876, the old-time nomadic, buffalo-hunting culture was gone.

War played an important part in Plains Indian culture, as shown in this painting called Indian Warfare *by Frederic Remington.*

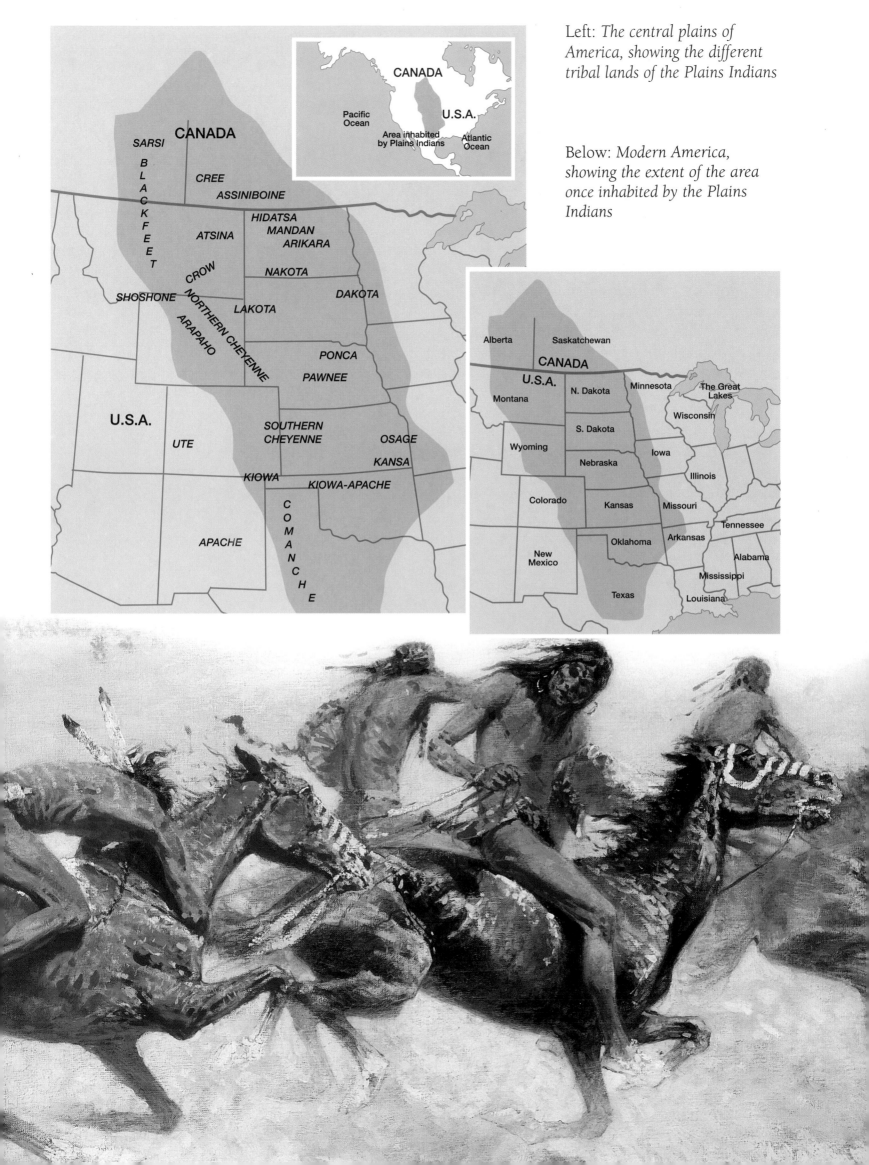

Left: *The central plains of America, showing the different tribal lands of the Plains Indians*

Below: *Modern America, showing the extent of the area once inhabited by the Plains Indians*

THE PLAINS INDIAN TRIBES

Although there were around thirty different tribes of Plains Indians, their total population was never more than 200,000 people. All the tribes spoke different languages, although some of them had similar words and sounds. Large tribes like the Sioux were divided into sub-tribes (the Lakota, Nakota, and Dakota Sioux), who in turn, were divided into smaller units who lived together called hunting bands. People could not marry anyone within the same band, and when a man married, he usually went to live with his wife's band.

Right: *Northern Cheyenne warrior. His shirt and leggings trimmed with human hair show that he is a war party leader.*

The Cheyenne

The Cheyenne moved onto the plains in the mid-1700s. In the 1820s, they divided into two groups, the Northern Cheyenne, who lived in the territories that are now Montana and Wyoming, and the Southern Cheyenne, who lived in what are now Oklahoma, Nebraska, Colorado, and Kansas. The whole Cheyenne population numbered around 3,000 people. From the 1830s, the Cheyenne became friendly with the people of the Lakota Sioux tribe. Their traditional enemies were the Ute, Pawnee, Crow, and Blackfeet.

The Lakota Sioux

The Lakota were one of the last tribal groups to move onto the plains, but they quickly adapted to their new lifestyle. They were a large and powerful tribe of about 12,000 people, who were very influential in both Plains Indian culture and politics.

Right: *This Lakota Sioux warrior carries a war party leader's lance and stone club. His headdress is made of ermine skins, buffalo horns, and eagle feathers.*

Left: *Southern Cheyenne Dogman. His headdress, rattle, paint design, and sash show that he is a member of the Dog Society, a police and military organization that became its own band within the Cheyenne nation.*

Above: *Southern Cheyenne woman. Holding her saddle and a painted buffalo robe, she is wearing her best clothes for a tribal celebration.*

Right and center: *Blackfeet Grizzly Bear Man*

Below: *This Crow Man is holding a combination pipe and tomahawk. His clothes show his exploits in battle; he has captured a gun and led war parties and horse-stealing raids.*

The Crow
Numbering around 4,000, the Crow were a very artistic people who lived along the Yellowstone River. Surrounded by their traditional enemies the Blackfeet, Cheyenne, Arapaho, and Sioux, the Crow became the allies of the white settlers.

Blackfeet chief

The Blackfeet

Like the Sioux, the Blackfeet were divided into three main groups. Numbering around 18,000 people, they dominated southern Alberta, Canada, and western Montana. This area had plenty of grass and water, and was one of the last places that herds of buffalo could be found. The Blackfeet fought against almost all the other tribes, with no allies except for the Sarsi (a small tribe of around 800 people) and sometimes the Atsina (3,000 people).

The Blackfeet had a Braves' Society that chose two men every year to serve as "Grizzly Bear Men." These men had to be fierce warriors who fought like grizzly bears, always charging at the enemy. On ceremonial occasions, or to go into battle, they wore bear-fur arm bands, bear-claw necklaces, a bear-fur belt, and a special headdress made from two grizzly claws.

Right: *This Blackfeet woman is holding a travois. The wooden A-frame platform is placed on the back of a horse or dog and loaded up with baggage, and when the animal moves forward the two poles are dragged along behind. The Plains Indians use these to transport their belongings from place to place.*

THE HORSE

Between 1.5 million and 600,000 years ago, the ancestors of modern horses migrated from Asia to the North American continent, traveling across the Bering Land Bridge, which joined the two land masses during this time. However, they became extinct in the New World, and were unknown to the Native peoples until they were reintroduced into Mexico by the Spaniards in the 1500s. As these horses were traded and captured, they began to move northward throughout America, and by the the mid-1700s, most of the Plains Indians had them.

The arrival of the horse transformed the lives of the Plains Indians, who had previously relied on dogs to carry their belongings as they moved around. Since horses can transport far heavier loads than dogs, the Plains Indians were able to make themselves bigger tipis and keep larger supplies of food. They were also able to travel farther and faster than ever before. Children became used to horses from an early age, and both boys and girls were taught to ride.

Below: *A man's saddle, made from a buffalo-hide pad stuffed with antelope or buffalo hair. The stirrups are made of green cottonwood and covered with rawhide. The saddle blanket, made from the skin of a mountain lion, is a prized item.*

Hunting with Horses

Although buffalo are large animals, they gallop fast, and hunting them on foot usually involved stampeding them over a cliff and taking those animals that were killed in the fall. The arrival of the horse meant that hunters could chase the buffalo herds, and each man could pick out one or two animals and shoot them. A fast and obedient horse was essential for success in hunting.

10

Horses in Warfare

A rich family might own as many as thirty horses, but only one or two would be good enough to be ridden into battle. For a warrior or a hunter, success depends on owning a fast, well-trained, long-winded, and brave horse. Good horsemanship is also very important. In battle especially, being able to stay on the horse's back means staying alive, while falling—or being dragged—off a horse would mean certain death.

The best riders rescue fallen comrades by lifting them onto their galloping horses in the thick of a battle. They protect themselves from bullets and arrows by slipping around to their horses' sides and hanging there.

Left: *A scarf or banner tied onto the warhorse's bridle shows that it has been ridden into battle before.*

An Indian family moving camp. One of the horses pulls a travois, laden with belongings.

Right: *Plains Indians either make their own bridles from braided buffalo hide or hair, or they use leather bridles with metal bits, bought from white traders.*

THE FAMILY

he year is 1868, and the Northern Cheyenne warrior Real Bird and his family live on the plains of southeastern Montana. Families are very important to the Plains Indian culture, and each member has a particular part to play. If a boy is successful as a warrior and hunter, or a girl as a homemaker and craftswoman, this will help to ensure the continued wealth and success of each family, and therefore of the tribe as a whole.

Above left: *Timber Leader, the grandfather, looks after the family's spiritual needs. He has been a great warrior, and young men come to him for advice and to listen to his stories of past battles.* Above right: *Brave Heart Woman, the grandmother, is an expert homemaker and craftswoman, and she is now passing on these skills to her granddaughters. She watches Real Bird's wives to make sure that they are doing their work properly.*

Polygamy

Real Bird is a polygamist, which means that he has more than one wife. Most of the men in his village have two or three wives, and very rich men have as many as eight. It is common for a man to marry two or three sisters.

One reason Plains Indians are polygamous is the war-like nature of their society. Hunting accidents and deaths in battle mean that there are fewer men than women. Women usually marry at fourteen or fifteen, and men when they are in their twenties.

Although wives contribute to the family's wealth by preparing buffalo hides for trade, they are not encouraged to have many children. It is hard to find food on the plains, and too many people would mean starvation for everyone.

Below: *Real Bird's two wives are Sees the Berries Woman (left) and Pretty Plume Woman (right). Sees the Berries Woman, a Southern Cheyenne, is the senior wife. She has a son, Rides the Herd (below right), age ten, and a daughter, Does Well (below center), age eight. Pretty Plume Woman's daughter, Two Whistles (below left), is six years old.*

Opposite: *Real Bird is an experienced hunter and provides well for his family. He is also a good trader and raises fine horses for racing and hunting.*

Above: *Real Bird's eldest child, Eagle that Sings, is the son of his first wife, who is dead. Now seventeen years old, Eagle that Sings must spend several years going on horse-stealing raids and war parties before he owns enough horses to be able to marry. Unlike his father, Eagle that Sings prefers the new style of dress, using some of the white man's clothes.*

THE VILLAGE

Almost all of the Plains Indians feed themselves by hunting, not farming, which means that they need to move from place to place. Each tribe is divided into several smaller groups called bands. Apart from certain times of year, when all the bands come together for ceremonies and celebrations, they live separately. Each band has to be small enough to move about fairly quickly and not use up too much food, but large enough to have enough men for a hunting party or to defend the village from enemy attack.

Right: *Setting up camp. Real Bird and the rest of his party have arrived in a new place. When the men have watered the horses, they relax and smoke their pipes, while the women set up the tipis (see page 16) and prepare the afternoon meal. After this, the children are allowed to play, and Real Bird and his wives can go and visit friends and other family members.*

Wickiups

Family tipis are often crowded places. In order to have their own space to sit and chat, young warriors like Eagle that Sings build themselves temporary brush-covered huts called wickiups.

Above: *The small bands of Plains Indians who travel together usually set up their tipis next to a river, if they can find one. If the whole tribe meet together for a ceremony, or if they suspect that there are enemies in the area, they lay the tipis out in concentric circles or one large circle. Tipis belonging to chiefs and warrior societies are often placed at the center of the village.*

Right: *When traveling, the Plains Indians pack their food and tools in cases called parfleches, which are made of folded and decorated buffalo hide.*

Traveling

Real Bird and his family are packed up and ready to move camp. They are waiting for the rest of the families in their band, because traveling in a very small family group is not safe.

During the winter, Plains Indians live in one camp for several months. Before moving they have a large tribal buffalo hunt. This ensures enough buffalo for a good supply of robes to trade and keep them warm, and plenty of meat dried and stored for the coming months.

In the spring, summer, and fall, the Real Bird family's band moves camp every few days. When traveling, they move slowly, covering eight to fifteen miles per day until they come to a place with fresh water, wood for their fires, and plenty of good grass for the horses.

SETTING UP A TIPI

P lains Indians need strong but lightweight dwellings that are easy to carry and erect, and buffalo-hide tipis are ideal for their nomadic lifestyle. In the days before horses, when the Plains Indians had only dogs to pull their loads, their tipis measured eight to twelve feet across. Since horses can carry more weight, with their arrival the tipis increased in size to about fourteen to seventeen feet across.

Traditionally, the family tipi, with its contents and furnishings, belongs to the women. It is their job to transport it and set it up on arrival at a new camp.

Left: *Tools for setting up a tipi. This cavalry feed bag contains wooden pegs to hold down the tipi cover and an elk-horn hammer to knock them into the ground. The thin sticks are lacing pins.*

Ceremonial Tipis

Besides family tipis there are also several larger tipis in each village where council and other meetings are held. These can be up to one hundred feet across. They can be made out of several buffalo-hide tipi covers stretched between poles in a circle or semicircle, or two large tipis can be set up facing each other, with a piece of hide stretched between them.

1 *The frame of the tipi is made of three or four wooden poles tied together with a rope. Once the frame is up, extra poles are leaned against the notch at the top of the tripod. Pretty Plume Woman ties strips of cloth to the tops of the poles to show which way the wind is blowing.*

2 *The remaining poles are added to the frame by leaning them against the central notch. When all the poles are in place, the women unpack the hide cover. Buffalo-hide covers can weigh up to 150 lbs., so the two women always work together.*

3 *The women fold the heavy tipi cover into a triangle and tie it to a pole that is placed on the ground. This last pole is then lifted into position at the back of the tipi, opposite where the tent flaps will be.*

4 *The women unfurl the cover (left), and pull it around the framework of poles.*

Smoke flap pocket

Smoke flap

Above: *Buffalo-hide tipi cover. Two semicircular pieces might be cut out for the door hole.*

Making a Tipi Cover

Tipis can be patched when they wear out, but industrious women like Sees the Berries Woman and Pretty Plume Woman replace their tipi at least every other year. They need eight to twenty tanned buffalo hides for a single tipi cover, and once they have scraped them clean, it takes one or two days to sew them together in a shape like the one shown. Women friends and relatives usually help each other.

Men who have earned battle honors often decorate the outer covers of tipis with pictures of their exploits or sacred symbols they have seen in dreams or visions.

5 *Small poles are inserted at the top of the tipi, creating small flaps called ears or women's arms. These can be adjusted to prevent drafts and allow the smoke from the fire in the center of the tipi to escape. When it rains, the flaps are closed so that the water runs down the outside of the tipi.*

INSIDE THE TIPI

M any family members live in one tipi, which becomes very crowded and allows for little privacy. As many as eleven adults and children can share a tipi, along with all of their clothing, tools, weapons, and food. The lack of space makes it essential to keep things very tidy, and everything and everyone has its proper place. The grandmother and the younger wives usually stay in the area where the food and firewood are kept and the cooking is done, and the man's senior wife sits at the rear of the tipi with her husband and his guests. The saddles and bridles are kept in the "men's side" of the tipi, and the men's weapons are always placed by their beds so that they can grab them quickly if the village is attacked during the night. Holy items are always placed at the rear of the tipi.

Right: *The interior of the Real Bird family's tipi. A well-furnished, highly decorated tipi like this one is the result of each family member working hard at his or her particular tasks. The tipis of less successful families, where the men are poor hunters and the women are not so skilled in crafts, are furnished with only the bare essentials.*

REAR OF TIPI

HOLY ITEMS

OWNER'S BED

BED

BED

FIRE

BED

BED

COOKING AREA

FRONT OF TIPI

Left: *Among the few pieces of furniture inside a tipi are backrests. These are made from peeled willow twigs and supported by wooden tripods. This one has a seat made from a blanket bought from a trader, a pillow stuffed with antelope fur, and a buffalo-calfskin head pad.*

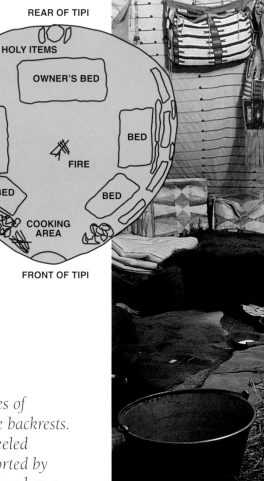

Tanning Hides

Buffalo hides are used to make both the outside of the tipi and interior furnishings such as blankets and parfleches, but they need to be tanned before use.

To prepare the hides, the women first stake them out on the ground and scrape both sides carefully with stone, bone, or metal tools, removing all the hair and any flesh that remains after the animal has been skinned. They then rub the hide with buffalo brains in order to soften it. Finally, they pull it back and forth across a rope made of buffalo sinew to keep it well stretched while it dries in the sun.

Above: *Tools for tanning hides: a buffalo leg bone "flesher" (left), an elk-horn hammer, and an elk-horn scraper (right).*

19

MORNING CHORES

I f Real Bird and Eagle that Sings are going hunting, or if the camp is being moved, it is necessary to make an early start. At other times, Sees the Berries Woman and Pretty Plume Woman get up first, in order to fetch wood and water and prepare the morning meal of boiled meat and broth. Anyone who has been out the night before, feasting, dancing, or visiting friends, sleeps in late, and on winter mornings, everyone is reluctant to leave the warm fire in the middle of the tipi and go out into the cold.

After bathing, Sees the Berries Woman and Pretty Plume Woman oil their hair, and sometimes their bodies, with melted bear fat. They then braid their hair before they begin the work of the day. In the summer months they try to do heavy work, like tanning hides, before the sun gets too hot.

Although some of the horses belong to individuals, including women and children, looking after them is men's work. As soon as they get up, Real Bird, Eagle that Sings, and Rides the Herd go to check on the horses, take them to the river for a drink, and maybe move them out to better grass. Horses are the most important and valuable of all the Plains Indians' possessions, so Real Bird has to be constantly on the lookout for thieves. If he suspects that there are raiding parties in the area, he tells the other men to wait until midday before moving their herds out to the prairies to graze.

Above: *Clothes for hunting, traveling, and work are usually simple and undecorated. Clothing for special occasions, such as battles or celebrations, is kept in beaded or porcupine-quilled saddle bags when it is not being worn.*

Right: *Personal items in everyday use (clockwise from top): a heavy knife with a beaded sheath, shell earrings, a trade bead and coin necklace, and a beaded amulet.*

Yucca Plants

Yuccas are used for different things: the fruit can be eaten and the spikey leaves *(see above)* and outer root used for firemaking tools. When it is peeled and soaked in water, the inner root *(see below)* makes excellent soap.

Left: *Rides the Herd bathes in the river before he goes to help the men water the horses.*

WOMEN'S WORK: FOOD

Real Bird and his family usually eat two meals a day, the first at mid-morning and the second in the late afternoon. These are prepared and served by Sees the Berries Woman, helped by Pretty Plume Woman and Brave Heart Woman. As most Plains Indian tribes do not grow their own crops, fruit, or vegetables, their diet is quite limited. Most of the food comes from the men's hunting, but the women gather wild foodstuffs such as berries, and barter for food with farming tribes or white traders.

The Plains Indians enjoy fresh meat and often eat it raw at the site of a kill. Inner organs are especially popular. Real Bird likes raw liver with bile from the gall bladder best, but nose gristle, fresh brains, and kidneys are all favorites. However, the Plains Indians' nomadic lifestyle means that many of their foods have to be dried so that they can be kept and transported from place to place. Meat and other foodstuffs are hung up in the hot sun until they are completely dried out and hard. They are later soaked or boiled in water to make them edible.

Real Bird's family has few eating utensils. If someone is invited to a feast, he is expected to bring his own knife, a carved wooden bowl, and a buffalo shoulder blade or scrap of rawhide to serve as a plate. Cups and spoons are carved from buffalo horn. Forks are unknown, and meat is eaten by first putting a piece in the mouth and then cutting it away from the rest of the lump with a knife. Meals are usually accompanied by a drink of water or meat broth.

Left: Besides fresh and dried meat, there are various other foods available (from top to bottom): bitter root; a braided string of dried prairie turnips; dried buffalo bladders for holding water; dried corn and rings of dried squash, both of which are obtained through tribes who come from the more fertile Missouri River area farther east; rosehips, eaten when food is scarce, set on a plate made from a buffalo shoulder blade; and dried chokecherries in a wooden bowl.

Above and left: *Pretty Plume Woman and Brave Heart Woman prepare and serve the afternoon meal.*

Below: *Women's tools for starting fires (clockwise from top left): a burning glass (magnifying glass); matches; a piece of flint; a knife in its sheaf; a bag to keep the smallest tools in, and some dried tinder. Matches, known as Lucifers because of a popular brand name, are a rare novelty on the prairies.*

WOMEN'S WORK: CRAFTS

ood wives like Sees the Berries Woman and Pretty Plume Woman are skilled in many different crafts. They make all of the clothing for their family, including moccasins, as well as saddles, packing gear, tipis, tipi furnishings, and various kinds of tools. Besides making everyday items, they have also mastered the traditional women's crafts such as beadwork, painting on rawhide, and porcupine-quill embroidery. These are mainly used to decorate clothes, because, like most nomadic peoples, the Plains Indians find this the easiest way to display their artistic achievements.

It is as important for a woman to be skilled in crafts as it is for a man to be a good hunter and a brave warrior. Sees the Berries Woman belongs to a special craftworkers' guild for women. Only the finest craftswomen are allowed to join. Membership of this guild gives Sees the Berries Woman high status in the tribe and the right to make certain religious items that other women are not allowed to make.

Above: *Woman's belt and knife with bead-embroidered sheath*

Right: *Sees the Berries Woman and Pretty Plume Woman teach their daughters how to sew.*

Beadwork

Glass beads like these, usually from Italy, are obtained at trading posts. They have to be strung on threads of buffalo sinew (*above*) one at a time.

MEN'S WORK: HUNTING

As the head of the family, Real Bird's chief responsibility is to provide meat and buffalo robes, since these are the things that allow them to have a comfortable life, with a large, well-furnished tipi and plenty of trade goods. The buffalo is the Plains Indians' most important quarry. In addition to the meat and hides, every other part of the animal, from the horns to the hoofs, is used by the Indians in their daily lives.

Above: *Every man needs a quirt, or whip, for his horse. For everyday use, a stick or buffalo tail will do. For special occasions, beaded wrist straps with elk horn or carved wooden handles are common.*

Center: *Buffalo with calf*

Right: *Tools for making weapons (from top to bottom): a sharpened stone knife; stone drill; metal, stone, and bone arrowheads; a sanding stone (right); a bundle of animal sinew, and a glue stick. Almost every hunter and warrior knows how to make his own bows and arrows. It is usually older men like Timber Leader who specialize in making them because the younger men are not always willing to do such time-consuming work. Eagle that Sings prefers to save his energy for hunting buffalo, and he will gladly trade meat and hides for new weapons.*

Above: *To hunt buffalo successfully on horseback with a bow and arrow, the rider needs to have good control over his horse.*

Left: *Men spend part of their leisure time making and repairing their weapons. Raw bow staves are carved into a rounded shape and backed with animal sinews to give them more power and strength. Bows can also be made from elk antlers and bighorn sheep horn.*

Right: *Arrows are painted with the owner's individual markings so that on a big hunt, each man can tell which animal he has shot.*

MEN'S WORK: PREPARING FOR BATTLE

A lthough Plains Indian tribes fight wars for the same reasons that cause many people to go into battle—to capture land and for revenge—war is also an important part of their culture and has both a ceremonial and a spiritual aspect.

Men are considered to be the protectors of the tribe and are expected to help defend the village. When Rides the Herd is thirteen, he will begin to learn the art of warfare by accompanying war parties. He will not fight, but he will fetch water, gather wood, and prepare meals for the adults. When he is seventeen, he will be invited to join his first war party as a warrior. Young warriors like Eagle that Sings go on horse-stealing expeditions and raids until they have enough wealth to marry.

When Eagle that Sings has proved that he is a good warrior, Real Bird will be able to retire from fighting. However, like Timber Leader, he will still consider himself to be a warrior, and he will always be prepared to fight to the death in order to defend the women and children.

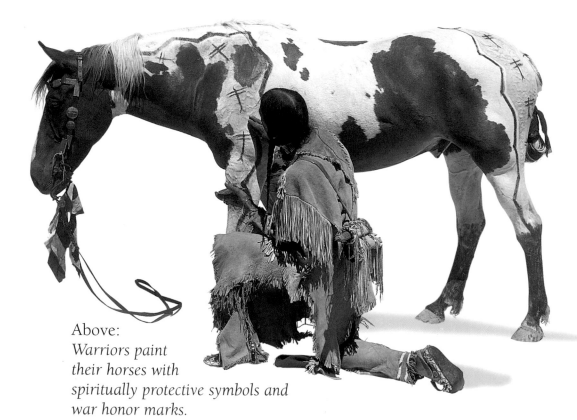

Above:
Warriors paint their horses with spiritually protective symbols and war honor marks.

28

Left: *The highest ranking warriors and chiefs hold meetings in a council, or warrior society, tipi. Each man's shield hangs above his seat. In pre-battle ceremonies, a man who wants to lead a war party offers his pipe to other warriors. If they smoke it, they have accepted his leadership for this battle.*

Protective Symbols
Pictures of animals, forces of nature, or the spirit world can be painted, beaded, quilled, carved, or formed from furs and hides in order to offer their owners spiritual protection both in battle and in their daily lives. They can be crafted onto clothes, weapons, and religious items, or painted directly onto a person's body.

Below (clockwise from center): *clamshell paint bowls and wolf moss for yellow dye; (above) buffalo-hoof paint bowl; small clamshell; three buffalo kneecap bone paint brushes; porcupine-tail hair brush; buffalo-horn powdered paint container; paint sticks; package of Chinese vermillion paint; three buckskin paint bags; three rock or earth pigments; rawhide painted case.*

MEN'S WORK: WARFARE

With their traditional enemies, the Plains Indians usually fight in small skirmishes, not large battles. This is more suited to their ideas about fighting, which do not include group discipline or following particular battle plans. What is important is individual combat and gaining as many "coups" or battle honors as possible. One method of "counting coup" is to touch an enemy with the hand, or a stick or quirt held in the hand, as a demonstration of personal bravery. Although the ideal is to touch a live, armed enemy, coup can also be counted on a dead or wounded man. For a warrior to have coup counted on him means a loss of status. Taking an enemy's horse or gun is also a major coup, and in some tribes it ranks higher than actually killing him.

Above: *This small pair of moccasins is a badge that shows that their owner has taken part in ten successful horse-stealing raids.*

Above center: *Shields are made out of rawhide from the thick neck or hump skin of an old buffalo bull. It is important for the rawhide to be thick to protect its owner from being wounded, but the symbols painted on the shield are more important, because they give spiritual protection in battle (see page 35).*

Left: *The gun is the Plains Indians' favorite weapon. A sawed-off .69 caliber flintlock musket like this one is very effective at short range and can easily be reloaded while on horseback. Guns are often decorated, and this one is ornamented with a recently taken scalp and some of the original gun owner's jewelry. The long-handled stone club is used in hand-to-hand fighting.*

Above and center: *A war party. War parties usually consist of the leader, his assistants, several scouts, and some warriors. The leader of a war party carries the pipe that he has used in the pre-battle ceremony. All the warriors who have smoked the pipe during the ceremony have accepted his leadership for that particular battle.*

CHILDREN

When a baby is born, its umbilical cord is cut and dried, then sealed in an amulet bag. This represents the child's connection to his or her mother, and, through her, to the rest of the tribe and the Great Spirit (*see page 34*). A respected relative or holy person is asked to name the child, and both boys and girls are given the names of famous ancestors or tribal heroes. A girl usually has one name, which does not change when she marries, but a boy may have several different names over the course of his life, which will either be given to him by others because of his exploits in battle, or revealed to him in a dream or spiritual vision (*see page 35*).

Left: *Throwing darts and "bull roarers" that can be whirled around to make a loud noise, are boys' games.*

Toys and Games

Plains Indian children's games are often an imitation of the roles that they will play as adults. Boys play at war and hunting, and girls play dollhouse with miniature tipis and dolls made out of sticks and scraps of cloth. Both boys and girls play ball and stick games similar to hockey or lacrosse, which are also enjoyed by adults.

Gambling games with counters and dice, like the one shown below left, are also popular with children. Adults often play for high stakes such as buffalo robes and horses.

Below: *Rides the Herd and his friends play a buffalo-hunting game, using hollow buffalo hoofs to represent adult buffalo, with buffalo-calf hoofs for the calves. Using buffalo toe bones, some of the boys pretend to be hunters. Chasing each other across the prairie, the boys practice the hunting skills they will need in years to come.*

Above: *While the boys play hunting games, Does Well and Two Whistles make a miniature village out of cottonwood leaves using split twigs for the horses and travois.*

Left: *Eagle that Sings's cedar love flute is precious and he keeps it in a specially painted buffalo rawhide case.*

Below: *A cut-off soldier's boot with the bottom sewn up makes a good place to keep the carved and painted sticks used in several gambling games.*

Courtship

Young warriors like Eagle that Sings spend a lot of their time in camp painting and dressing up to show off in front of the girls. After getting a girl's attention, a young man lets his intentions be known by singing flattering songs about her or sitting outside her family's tipi for hours, playing his love flute *(top center)*, which is believed to be able to entrance any girl its player fancies.

Eagle that Sings has fallen in love with Otter Horse Woman, and has obtained permission from her family to visit her in her tipi. They stand together in the doorway, and Eagle that Sings covers both of their heads with a large blanket so that they can talk in private. Unmarried girls are not allowed to talk to men on their own, so Otter Horse Woman's grandmother, mother, or aunt are always nearby.

33

MEDICINE

T he Plains Indians believe that everything in the world is part of one Great Spirit and is therefore a potential source of spiritual power. They call this power medicine.

Among most tribes there are two sorts of healers; in some cases one person fills both positions. Doctors charge a fee to splint broken bones, apply poultices, prescribe certain herbs, or sew up large wounds. They often make a theatrical display of their treatment in order to convince the patient of their power and to provide entertainment.

Holy people, known as medicine men or women, attend to the spiritual needs of others with their special powers, which are believed to have been given to them by the Great Spirit in dreams or visions.

Right: *Bears are believed to have great powers of healing. Timber Leader wears a bearskin to give him some of that power.*

Medicine Objects

Each person has special holy objects such as the quilled medicine pouch, sacred stick, and rattle shown here *(left)*, which provide inspiration and help to protect from harm. A holy person can tell someone which items to put into his or her medicine bag, or the affected individual may receive guidance in a spiritual vision. A medicine object is not simply special because of its shape or material. It has to be made sacred by being blessed by a holy person or used in a spiritual ceremony.

Death
Dead people are dressed in their finest clothes to prepare them for the journey into the next world. Their medicine objects, food, and—if they are male— sometimes their weapons, are wrapped up beside them in a buffalo robe. Most tribes then place the corpse on top of a scaffold that is raised about six feet off the ground. Eventually, the bones are removed and placed in crevices in the rocks.

The Vision Quest

Spiritual power is usually sought in a ritual in which the person seeking aid goes on a vision quest. He leaves the village and fasts and prays for up to four days in the hope of receiving a sign from God, which may come in the form of an animal, bird, rock, or tree, because the Great Spirit can communicate with people in any form at all. These visions are then interpreted by a holy person.

Dreams in normal sleep are also considered to be spiritually important and a source of power. A man may paint a symbol or animal that he has seen in a dream onto his shield to protect him in battle.

Above: *Sweat lodges are built from wooden poles covered in buffalo hides and are used for purification ceremonies. Water is poured onto hot stones in the center of the lodge to create steam. The men purify themselves physically and spiritually by sweating.*

GOVERNMENT, GATHERINGS, AND FESTIVALS

Most Plains Indian tribes select their leaders. Older men like Timber Leader serve as civil chiefs, making decisions about village matters, and younger men like Real Bird are the warrior leaders, deciding when it is right to go to war. Although women's opinions are respected, they are usually voiced by their husbands.

Many tribal gatherings are combinations of social and religious celebrations, with dancing, storytelling, feasting, gift-giving, courting, speeches, and games. Gatherings usually take place in the summer, when it is easier to travel and there is plenty of food for everyone and grass for the horses. Most gatherings last about a week, which is as long as the available grass and fuel last.

Below: *The pipe stem (top left) is decorated with porcupine quills, and next to it is the carved stone pipe bowl. Below them are the beaded bag where they are stored, bags of tobacco, a buffalo shoulder-blade tobacco board colored with sacred red earth paint, and some pipe tools.*

Right: *Real Bird's brother Enters the Medicine Lodge prepares his shield and "medicine bundle" of holy objects for a ceremony by turning them to face the sun so that they can absorb its power.*

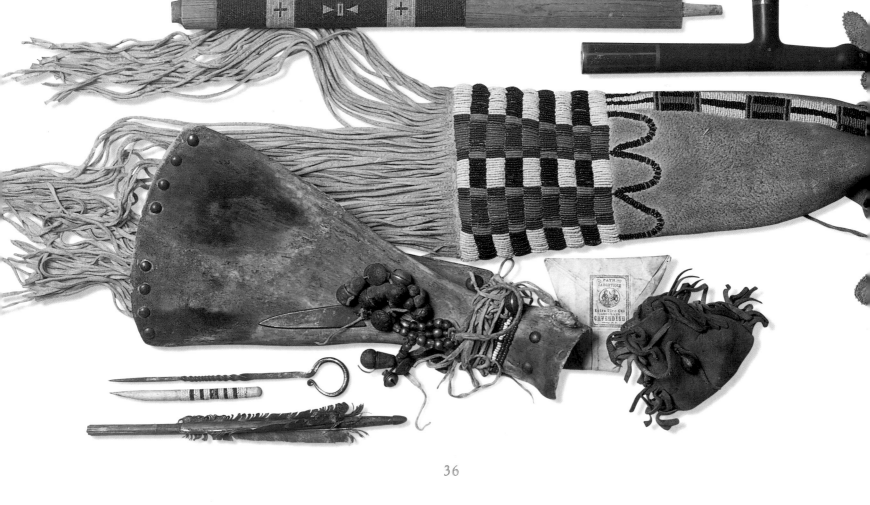

Smoking

Pipe smoking plays an important part in spiritual ceremonies. There are specially decorated sacred pipes for this purpose, as well as plain ones for social smoking. In many tribes, it is common for both men and women to smoke a mixture of tobacco and herbs. This combination is thought to represent all the living things in the world, and the pipe is symbolic of the flesh and blood of human beings. The act of smoking brings the elements together. The smoke from the pipe can represent a prayer, a gift, or a request for aid from the Great Spirit.

Right: *This piece of dried buffalo dung (top center) is used as an altar for the preparation of incense, which is made by burning sage, sweet grass, or other herbs. The hollow buffalo hoofs are used to mix sacred paint.*

Dances

Dancing is a very important part of the Plains Indians' ceremonial, spiritual, and social life. It is thought to renew the earth's spirit, the animals and crops, and maintain the energy and lifeforce of the tribe. Everyone, from the very young to the very old, is expected to dance, and both warrior societies and women's guilds host their own dances.

Scalp dances, which can last many days, are held as victory celebrations over enemies. The buffalo dance *(above)*, which depicts a hunt, is performed by men wearing buffalo head masks. It is danced when meat is scarce, in order to bring the herds closer to the village. During the dance, young men leave the village in search of the herds.

TRADE

The Plains Indians have a long tradition of trading, both with each other and with white people. When the Plains Indians first came into contact with white traders and settlers, they soon figured out that the traders' metal axes, kettles, and guns could make their lives easier, and just like any other people they liked to have new clothes and jewelry.

Horses are the most valuable items that Plains Indians like Real Bird and his family have to offer for trade. One warhorse is worth

ten saddle horses, and one racing horse is worth ten guns. A saddle horse is usually worth one gun with one hundred rounds of ammunition or eight buffalo robes. A single buffalo robe can be swapped for three metal knives or twenty-five rounds of ammunition, but a person who wants a gun needs to give the trader eight or ten buffalo robes. If the buffalo robe is finely decorated, it may be worth as much as three packhorses. Real Bird also offers the traders wolf and beaver fur and pemmican, which is a specific type of food made from dried meat mixed with dried berries and covered in melted fat. Pemmican is very useful to people who live on the plains because it can be kept for a long time.

White traders also offer the Plains Indians seashells and beads for making jewelry, and shell-and-bone hair pipes, such as those shown on the breastplate above. These popular accessories are manufactured thousands of miles away by white workers in New Jersey. The Plains Indians also trade dried buffalo meat, dried vegetables, clothing, and regalia.

Trade goods are imported from all over the world: glass beads from Italy, bright red paint from China, guns and cloth from Britain, and seashells from the Pacific coast and Russia.

Right: *As well as guns and ammunition, white traders offer items such as these (clockwise from left): brass thimbles for sewing and decoration; tweezers for plucking facial hair; metal knives; tobacco cans; coffee; blocks of tea; packets of tobacco; matches; "burning" or magnifying glasses for starting fires, and mirrors.*

Above: *The Indians quickly adapt items offered by white traders for their own use. For example, this soldier's ammunition box and tin for percussion caps have been turned into jewelry boxes.*

Above: *Brass rings from France and rings with glass stones are cheap but very popular.*

Traveling Traders

White traders like this man travel from village to village. Others set up permanent shops called trading posts. During the nineteenth century, more and more of these were established, especially by the fur companies, who came to rely heavily on the Indian trappers and hunters. Men and women soon learned how to spot poorly made goods and how to get a good deal.

The trader shown above is well known to the Real Bird family, as he is married to a woman from their village. This often happens—the life of a trader who travels by himself is lonely, and marriage to a Plains Indian woman can help to create friendly relations with his customers.

LEISURE TIME

In the summertime, almost everyone in the village is busy with some task, construction project, or with preparations for a ceremony or festival. The women are especially busy, but they still manage to find some time to relax by visiting friends, storytelling, and playing games. Many adults stay up late, sometimes all night, attending dances and other social functions.

Winter is the time for relaxing, catching up on craft projects, and trying to stay warm and well fed while using up as little energy as possible. After sunset, the fires in the tipis are the only source of light and heat. The beds, made of buffalo robes, are soft, warm, and comfortable. The time for action will come again with the spring, when the cycle will renew itself, as it has done forever.

Right: *Both men and women enjoy gambling. Dice are made from carved bone or painted plum seeds. European playing cards, bought from traders, are also popular.*

Above: Real Bird entertains his friends with stories of his heroic war deeds, which he has painted on a buffalo robe. This is called a pictograph, and it is one of the ways in which Plains Indians record their history.

Below: Watercolors, crayons, chalk, and colored pencils are all traded and used to make pictographs. This one has been painted in a white man's business ledger.

Above: Brave Heart Woman tells a story to her grandchildren before they go to bed. Those who have lived long lives are thought to have a lot of wisdom, and it is their duty to pass on the tribal history to the next generation.

Left: Almost everybody turns out to watch horseracing, which is a very popular sport. Like a good warhorse or hunting horse, a fast racehorse is worth a lot to its owner.

SOLDIERS AND SETTLERS

The nomadic, horseback culture of the Plains Indians lasted for approximately 150 years, and only during the last 25 were there open conflicts with outsiders. The first white men to arrive on the western plains were fur trappers. Known as mountain men, their relationship with the Plains Indians was usually friendly, and many learned to speak Indian languages. The Indians also got on well with the white traders, and they were able to benefit from new goods such as guns and metal cooking utensils. When the first pioneers and soldiers came, as long as there were plenty of buffalo and the newcomers did not want to settle on their land and fence it off, the Plains Indians were happy both to tolerate their presence and to engage in trade. New diseases brought by the white people, however, such as measles, smallpox, and cholera, killed many Plains Indians, and the white man's drink, alcohol, also took its toll. White and Indian hunters alike slaughtered the buffalo herds: when white men first arrived, there were 40 million or more buffalos in the North American continent, but by 1890 fewer than 1,000 were left.

The white farmers who came to the plains wanted the land where the Indians had traditionally lived and hunted. During the Indian Wars (1854–1890) many of the Plains Indians were forced to move into special areas called reservations. Some of these were on their homelands, but some tribes were made to move far away to poor land, which the farmers did not want.

Above right: *A painting of Fort Laramie, Wyoming, by Alfred Jacob Miller. The fort was established in 1834 by the American Fur Trading Company to buy animal pelts from mountain men and Indian trappers. In 1849 the army took it over to guard and service the wagon trail roads that were used by immigrants and gold rushers heading for California.*

Above: *Although this photograph is called* Sunset of a Dying Race, *the Plains Indians did not die out. They have adapted their culture to the modern world.*

Plains Indian Culture

This photograph shows children arriving at an Indian Training School. Schools like this one attempted to civilize the Indians and convert them to Christianity. The children were dressed in white people's clothes and forbidden to speak their native languages.

Despite problems of racism and poverty, however, Plains Indian culture has survived. Its languages are still spoken, and the Indian population of North America, which was down to 250,000 in 1900, had risen to around 2 million by 1990.

THE VILLAGE IN TIME

H ere are some of the events that took place in American history before, during, and after the period when Real Bird and his family lived on the plains of Montana.

1000 Many great cultures and civilizations flourish and fade away before the first Norsemen make contact with the Native peoples of North America.

1492 Columbus, believing he has found a new route to the Indies, "discovers" the New World and calls its inhabitants Indians.

1493 Columbus returns to the New World with 19 stallions and 23 mares.

1519–1540 Spanish explorers Cortez and DeSoto travel and raid their way through Central America and the southern states of North America.

1600–1700 Plains of North America very sparsely populated. Eastern woodland tribes begin to obtain firearms and push weaker, unarmed tribes out of their homelands.

1720–1730 Tribes venturing out onto the prairies begin to obtain horses, guns, and metal utensils.

1750–1760 Almost all tribes now living on the plains are immigrants from further east who have taken up the nomadic, horseback buffalo-hunting culture.

1779–1781 Smallpox epidemic

1800–1830 Fur-trade era begins. Many areas over-hunted and trapped by Indian and white trappers alike.

1804–1806 The Lewis and Clark Expedition explores the Upper Missouri and Oregon territory.

1805–1807 Zebulon Pike searches for the source of the Mississippi and explores the Rocky Mountains.

1811 John Jacob Astor establishes a fur-trading post in Oregon.

1830 Congress passes the Indian Removal Act, giving President Jackson the power to remove Native Americans from the East to lands west of the Mississippi.

1830–1870 Buffalo hide trade era: millions of animals killed in order to trade them for guns, metal tools, beads, alcohol, and other trade items.

1833 Bent's Fort built in southern Colorado for fur trade with the southern and central Plains Indians.

1836–1840 Smallpox epidemic

1842–1845 John Fremont maps the West.

1843 First wagon train crosses continent to Oregon.

1845 John L. O'Sullivan writes of the United States' "Manifest Destiny" to expand across the continent.

1847 Marcus and Narcissa Whitman and 12 other settlers are massacred by Cayuse Indians at their mission in Oregon; the U.S. Army is brought in with the aim of protecting the settlers.

1848 Mexico cedes California and the Southwest to the United States. Gold is discovered in California, leading to the 1849–50 Gold Rush.

1849 Fort Laramie, a U.S. Army post, is established at old Fort William in Wyoming, a fur-trading post. Its purpose is to protect wagon train and Gold Rush immigrants.

1851 Treaty made at Fort Laramie with Northern Plains tribes. Indians promise not to attack overland routes in return for cloth and food and other amenities.

1853 Same treaty at Fort Atkinson with southern tribes.
Fort Riley established in Kansas.

1854 A white settler complains that Sioux Indians butchered one of his cattle. Soldiers investigate and open fire on the Indian camp. The Indians retaliate, killing Lieut. Grattan and 28 men in what becomes known as the Grattan Massacre. Thereafter attacks on overland routes resume. The Kansas-Nebraska Act formally opens these territories to white settlers.

1856 Smallpox epidemic

1857–1878 Wars between the Plains Indians and U.S. soldiers.

1851–1880s Many treaties signed and reservations of land allotted to various Indian tribes.

1861-1862 Smallpox epidemic

1861-1865 American Civil War

1864 Massacre of Sand Creek: U.S. soldiers kill at least 150 Cheyenne and Arapaho, mostly women and children.
State of Nevada joins the Union.

1866 Forts Reno, Phil Kearny, and C. F. Smith are built to protect the Bozeman Trail.

1866–1868 Red Cloud leads the Oglala Sioux into war against the U.S. Army over the Bozeman Trail area. The government agrees to evacuate forts along the trail.

1868 Real Bird and family are living on the plains of Montana.
Fort Laramie treaty of 1851 is renegotiated. Lands contested between the U.S. government and the Lakota given to the Lakota.

1869 First American transcontinental railroad is completed.
The Battle of Summit Springs, Colorado; the power of the Southern Cheyenne Dogmen is broken.

1871 Fort Abraham Lincoln is built in North Dakota to protect railroads.

1874 Fort Robinson is built in Nebraska to watch over the Lakota reservations.

1876 Battle of the Little Bighorn: Sioux and Cheyenne warriors defeat General Custer's troops.
State of Colorado joins the Union.

1877 Chief Joseph of the Nez Perce surrenders to the U.S. Cavalry.
Crazy Horse of the Oglala Lakota surrenders and four months later is killed resisting arrest.

1878–1886 The last of the great buffalo herds destroyed and with them the 150-year period of the mounted Plains Indian culture.

1881 Sitting Bull of the Hunkpapa Lakota surrenders.

1887 Buffalo Bill's Wild West Show performs for Queen Victoria in Great Britain.

1889 Two million acres of Indian territory (Oklahoma) are opened to white settlers. States of Montana, North Dakota, and South Dakota join the Union.

1890 Battle of Wounded Knee: the end of the American-Indian wars.
Sitting Bull killed by Indian police.
States of Idaho and Wyoming join the Union.

1896 State of Utah joins the Union.

1899 State of Washington joins the Union.

GLOSSARY

Amulet A small religious item, like a charm, which has spiritually protective qualities. The Plains Indians wore amulets in their hair, on their bodies, or attached to their clothing or horse harness.

Buffalo robe A tanned buffalo hide with the hair left on to give it extra warmth. Robes were used for bedding and swapped for trade goods.

Cottonwood A large hard-wood tree used in the construction of saddles, bowls, clubs, and many other items. The bark from the upper branches was used as food for horses in winter.

Elk A very large member of the deer family found in the western states of America.

Flintlock A front-loading gun used by many soldiers and Indians in the nineteenth century. When a flintlock gun is fired, the flint strikes an L-shaped piece of metal called a frizzen and makes a spark. This ignites the gunpowder in the gun's pan and causes the powder inside the gun to explode, firing the shot.

Great Spirit One of several names for the supreme deity worshiped by the Plains Indians. Other names were All-Being, Mysterious One, Grandfather, and Old Man.

Medicine Holy power. A medicine man or woman is someone who is known to have this power.

Nomads Peoples who have portable homes and roam from place to place over a large area, looking for food and grazing.

Parfleche Any untanned or rawhide material folded to make a carrying case, from a French word meaning to parry, or turn, an arrow.

Pictograph Stylized drawings painted in pigments (*see below*) on tipis and clothing.

Pigment A natural or man-made substance used for coloring or dyeing clothing, tipis, and horse equipment. Plains Indians applied pigment to their skin both in the form of decoration and to help prevent sunburn.

Prairie The large, grassy level or slightly rolling area of land of the Missouri-Mississippi valley. It has few trees but rich soil and enough rain for growing grain crops. On its west side, the prairie merges with the high plains, where lack of rain makes the land more suitable for grazing animals than raising crops.

Rawhide An animal hide that has been scraped clean on both sides (flesh and hair), and then stretched and dried to a semi-rigid consistency.

Reservation An area of land set aside for use by specific Indian tribes or nations.

Scout A guide. Scouts, who knew the land well, traveled ahead of hunting or war parties looking for the quarry such as buffalo herds or the enemy. They then reported to the party's leader.

Settler In the 1850s and '60s, these pioneers, also known as overlanders, left settled parts in the East to go and build new homes in the West, which was only just being acquired by the U.S. government. They traveled in large groups in a line of covered wagons known as wagon trains.

Sinew Animal tendons used as thread for sewing, binding, and repairing various items.

Tipi A conically shaped, portable tent made of buffalo hides, elk hides, or canvas. (A wigwam, sometimes confused with a tipi, is a a bark-covered hut.)

Travois An A-shaped apparatus made of poles of wood, which was attached to a horse's back and used to haul heavy loads.

Yucca A large plant with stiff, swordlike leaves branching from a central stalk. It was used for firemaking tools, and for soap. The soft, nut-flavored seed could be eaten.

Places to Visit and Acknowledgments

Forts

Bent's Old Fort National Historic Site
35110 Highway 194 East, La Junta, Colorado 81050-9523
Telephone: (719) 384-2596

Fort Fetterman Historic Site
752 Highway 93, Douglas, Wyoming 82633
Telephone: (307) 684-7629

Fort Laramie National Historic Site
National Park Service HC 72 Box 389,
Fort Laramie, Wyoming 82212
Telephone: (307) 837-2221

Fort Larned National Historic Site
Route 3, Larned, Kansas 67550
Telephone: (316) 285-6911

Fort Phil Kearney State Historic Site
P.O. Box 520, Story, Wyoming 82842
Telephone: (307) 684-7629

Fort Union Trading Post National Historic Site
15550 Highway 1804, Williston, North Dakota 58801
Telephone: (701) 572-9083

Museums

National Museum of the American Indian
Alexander Hamilton U.S. Customs House,
1 Bowling Green, New York, New York 10004
Telephone: (212) 668-6624

Buffalo Bill Historical Center
720 Sheridan Avenue, Cody, Wyoming 82414
Telephone: (307) 587-4771

Colorado Historical Society
1300 Broadway, Denver, Colorado 80203
Telephone: (303) 866-3682

Knife River Indian Village National Historical Site
P.O. Box 9, 4201 Stanton, North Dakota 58571
Telephone: (701) 745-3309

Little Bighorn Battlefield National Monument
P.O. Box 39, Crow Agency, Montana 59022
Telephone: (406) 638-2621

Oregon Trail Interpretive Center
P.O. Box 987, Baker City, Oregon 97814
Telephone: (541) 523-1843

Museum of the Plains Indians
P.O. Box 410, Browning, Montana 59417
Telephone: (406) 338-2230

Acknowledgments
Breslich & Foss would like to thank Kennard Real Bird, Jack Real Bird, Jim Real Bird, Henry Real Bird, Ramona R. Real Bird, Shawn Real Bird, John Real Bird, Mark Real Bird, Polly Real Bird, Lucy Lee Real Bird, James Real Bird, Sloane Real Bird, Jessi Real Bird, Terry Anna Cummins, Nicole Cummins, Kordell Cummins, Brandon Yellow Wings, Hartford Lee Bear Claw, Tiffany Glenn, and Roy Martin for acting as models and for the use of their land and horses.

Picture Credits
Thomas Gilcrease Institute of American History and Art, Tulsa Oklahoma: pp.4–5 (bottom)
Glenbow Archives, Calgary Alberta: p.4, ref. NA-936-34 (top right)
Joslyn Art Museum, Nebraska: pp.42–3 (top center)
National Anthropological Archives, Smithsonian Institution: pp.42–3 (bottom center), p.43 (top right)
Princeton Collection of Western Americana: p.43 (bottom center)
Royal Canadian Mounted Police Centennial Museum: p.4 (top right)

All clothing, regalia, tipi furnishings, and horse equipment made by Michael Bad Hand Terry, except: tipi interior, pp.18–19, beaded moccasins, p.24, and paint bag, p.29, by Roy Martin; large grizzly bear claw necklace, p.34, by John Arrasmith; and painted rawhide bags pp.15, 39, and 40, by Ivan Hankla.

Village set technicians and assistants: Jason White Dog Terry and Silas Sky Mentzer.

Landscapes, tipi interiors, and artifacts were photographed at the Little Bighorn Battlefield site at Gerryowen, Montana.